# A YEAR IN A
# Village

by Sally Hewitt
Photographs by Chris Fairclough

W
## FRANKLIN WATTS
LONDON•SYDNEY

This edition 2008
First published in 2004 by Franklin Watts
338 Euston Road, London Nw1 3BH

Franklin Watts Australia
Level 17/207, Sydney, NSW 2000

© Franklin Watts 2004


Editor: Kate Newport
Art director: Jonathan Hair
Designer: Steve Prosser

Photographs:
Bridget Sherlock: 6, 9, 10; Robert Pickett: 16 (inset).
All other photography by Chris Fairclough.

A CIP catalogue record for this book
is available from the British Library

ISBN 978 0 7496 8308 5

Printed in Malaysia

Franklin Watts is a division of Hachette
Children's Books, an Hachette Livre UK company.

# CONTENTS

# Spring

It is Spring in the village.

The post van arrives early at the village shop.

School children do Spring
projects in the woods.

There is plenty of water
in the village pond.

Spring is a busy
time for gardeners.

# Guests throw confetti at a Spring wedding.

Under the church roof,
baby birds wait for food.

# Summer

A splash in the paddling pool is fun in the Summer.

The cricket match goes
on all afternoon.

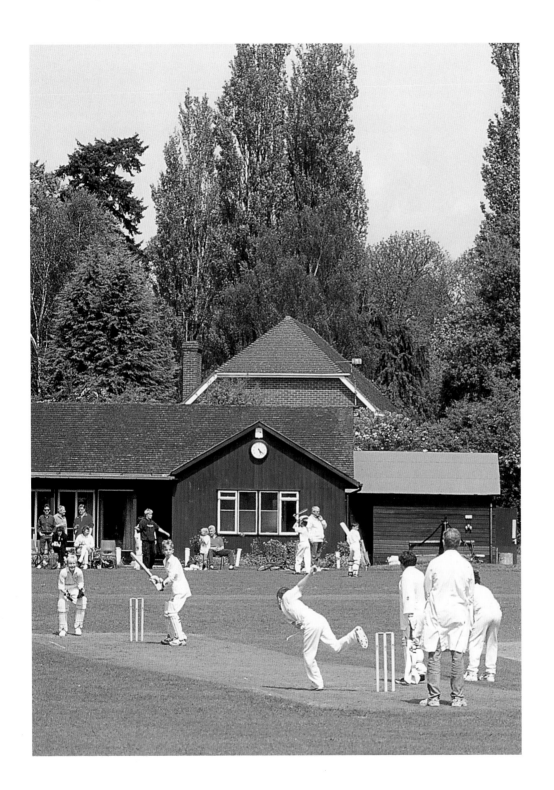

Everyone goes to the
Summer fête.

You can play on the bouncy
castle with your friends.

Water is low in
the village pond.

Insects buzz
around the
water's edge.

You can buy drinks and ice cream at the village shop.

# Autumn

At the Harvest display,
Autumn colours are bright.

Children make
Halloween
pumpkins.

Trees around the village
pond lose their leaves.

Piles of leaves are burnt on Autumn bonfires.

You can collect shiny conkers
and play with your friends.

It's time to play football
on the village green.

You have to wrap up in
coats and scarves to go to
school.

# Winter

In the Winter, the village pond freezes over...

...and the ducks have nowhere to swim.

Nuts and seeds will feed
the hungry birds.

The village is
covered in snow.

Children make snowmen
and have snowball fights.

It's cold and slippery
outside in the street.

# The children rehearse for their Nativity play.

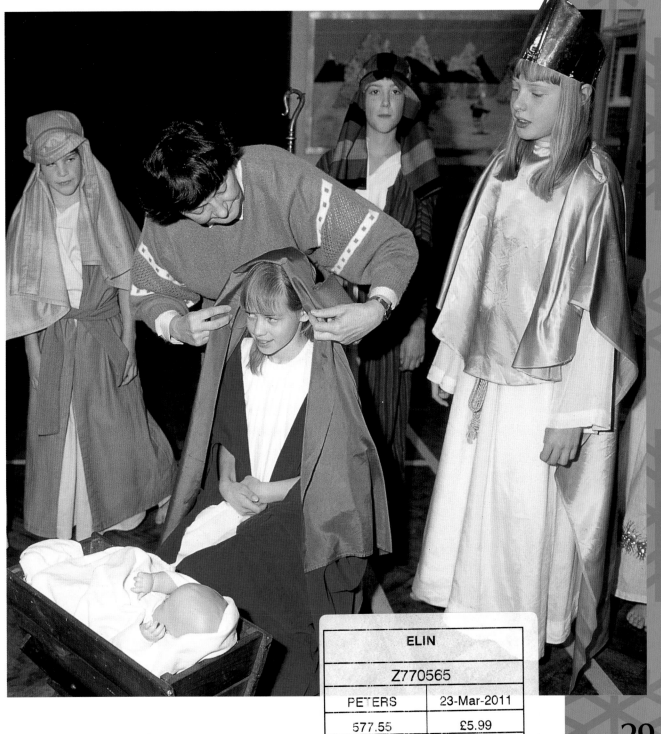

29

# INDEX